Michael Hague's
Little Treasury of Christmas Carols

Michael Hague's
Little Treasury of Christmas Carols

Illustrated by
MICHAEL HAGUE

A Galahad Book for Children

First Galahad Books edition published in 1997.

Galahad Books
A division of BBS Publishing Corporation
386 Park Avenue South
New York, NY 10016

Galahad Books is a registered trademark of BBS Publishing Corporation.

Published by arrangement with Henry Holt and Company, Inc.

Library of Congress Catalog Card Number: 97-71145

ISBN: 1-57866-001-7

Designed by Marc Cheshire.
Printed in China

Contents

Deck the Halls

Deck the halls with boughs of holly,
Fa la la la la, la la la la.

'Tis the season to be jolly,
Fa la la la la, la la la la.

Don we now our gay apparel,
Fa la la, la la la, la la la.

Troll the ancient Yuletide carol,
Fa la la la la, la la la la.

See the blazing Yule before us,
Fa la la la la, la la la la.

Strike the harp and join the chorus,
Fa la la la la, la la la la.

Follow me in merry measure,
Fa la la, la la la, la la la.

While I tell of Yuletide treasure,
Fa la la la la, la la la la.

Fast away the old year passes,
Fa la la la la, la la la la.

Hail the new, ye lads and lasses,
Fa la la la la, la la la la.

Sing we joyous all together,
Fa la la, la la la, la la la.

Heedless of the wind and weather,

Fa la la la la, la la la la!

Jingle Bells

Dashing through the snow,
in a one-horse open sleigh,

O'er the fields we go,
laughing all the way.

Bells on bobtail ring,
making spirits bright.

Oh, what fun it is to sing
a sleighing song tonight!

Oh! Jingle bells! Jingle bells!
Jingle all the way!

Oh, what fun it is to ride
in a one-horse open sleigh, hey!

Jingle bells! Jingle bells!
Jingle all the way!

Oh, what fun it is to ride
in a one-horse open sleigh!

HEY!

O Christmas Tree

O Christmas Tree,
O Christmas Tree,
Forever green
your branches!

How bright
in summer's sun
they glow,

How warm they shine
in winter's snow.

O Christmas Tree,
O Christmas Tree,
Forever green
your branches!

O Christmas Tree,
O Christmas Tree,
You give us so much
pleasure.

A grove of fir trees
standing near
Brings joy and beauty
through the year.

O Christmas Tree,
O Christmas Tree,
You give us so much
pleasure.

O Christmas Tree,
O Christmas Tree,
Your faith is strong
and steadfast.

It teaches us fidelity
And courage through
adversity.

O Christmas Tree,
O Christmas Tree,
Your faith is strong
and steadfast.

We Wish You a Merry Christmas

We wish you a merry Christmas,
we wish you a merry Christmas,
we wish you a merry Christmas
and a happy New Year!

Glad tidings we bring

to you and your kin,

*G*lad tidings for Christmas

and a happy New Year!

Please bring us some figgy pudding,

Please bring us some figgy pudding,

*P*lease bring us some figgy pudding,

and bring it right now!

We won't go until we get some,

We won't go until we get some,

We won't go until we get some,

so bring it right now!

We wish you a merry Christmas,

we wish you a merry Christmas,

we wish you a

Merry Christmas

and a

Happy New Year!